It is NOT Okay

to Disobey!

Story and Photography
by
Patty J. Keith

This book is dedicated to the precious children
at Heritage Church in Franklin, Tennessee.
I pray that you will always obey God
and seek Him first.
Everything else will fall right into place.
P.J.K.

Special "Thank YOU" to Jerry and Linda Gregg for providing the perfect landscape for Susie Mallard's (aka Thelma) nest each year.

Dandelion art by Brent Alan Wright - my precious son

Original oil art by Suzanne Gaudette Way, copyright 2011

Scripture quotations marked (TLB) are taken from The Living Bible copyright © 1971. Used by permission of Tyndale House Publishers, Inc., Carol Stream, Illinois 60188. All rights reserved.

Scripture quotations are from The Holy Bible, English Standard Version® (ESV®), copyright © 2001 by Crossway, a publishing ministry of Good News Publishers. Used by permission. All rights reserved

Visit "Duck Ponder Series" on Facebook for information on new releases.

PRINTED IN THE UNITED STATES OF AMERICA

Duck Ponder Series: Book VI, ISBN : 978-0-9893303-6-7

Children, obey your parents in everything, for this pleases the LORD.

Colossians 3:20 (ESV)

OUR FAMILY

Kaitlyn—Lia—Liam—Luke—Macy—Madeline—MaryKate—Mason

Brewer—Carley—Carson—Chris—Dylan—Ellie—Enoch—Isaac—Jonathan

Mia—Michael—Molly—Owen—Pierce—Sammy—Sophie—Thomas—Will

new baby ducklings

Susie and Drake Mallard are the proud parents of 14 baby ducklings.

Ponder this:
A male mallard is called a "drake" and a female mallard is called a "susie".

Susie will tell you that it is not easy
keeping count of her large brood.

Each and every little duckling is equally special to
her the same way we are all special to God.

Susie knew that one of her brood was strong willed and curious from the very day he was born.

Jonah did not want anyone to tell him what to do - not even his own mother.

Jonah had his own plans.
Jonah did not want to obey his mother.
Jonah thought it would be boring to follow his mother
around all day long.

So he decided that as soon as possible
he would go his own way.

Jonah knew that his sister Eve was easily persuaded so he asked her to go with him.

Jonah and Eve had big plans to explore this new world. No one was going to stand in their way!

So one day when all the ducklings went out for a swim

Ponder this:
Ducklings swim the first day out of their nest but can not fly until they are a couple of months old.

Jonah and Eve slipped away from their mother and the 12 other ducklings.

Basking in the sun, Susie did not notice
that Jonah and Eve were not with her brood
until her friend Jack, the Pekin duck,
shouted to her from the bank.

Susie Mallard immediately
came out of the water
and onto the bank to count
the ducklings for herself.

But sadly, she too only saw 12.

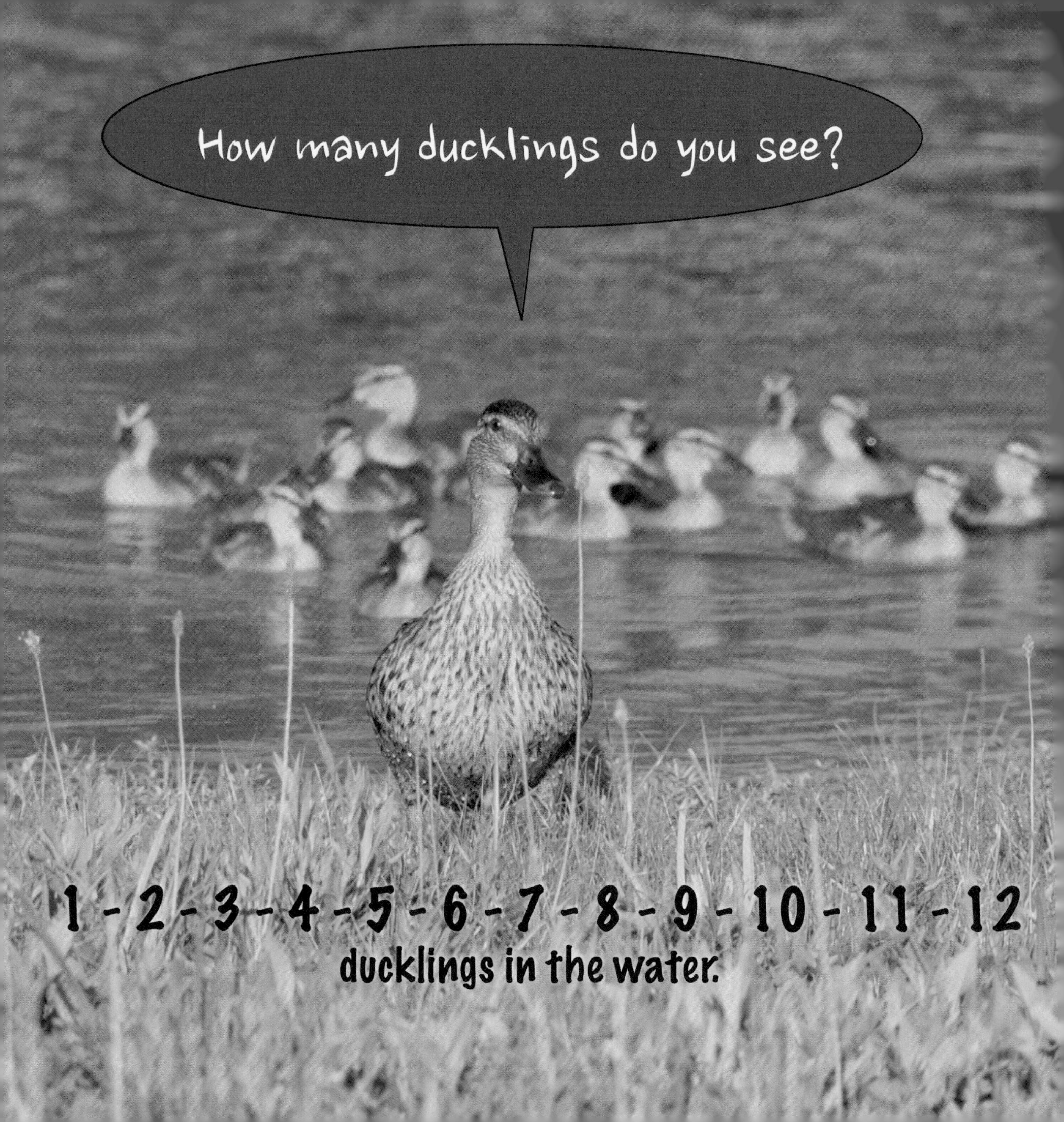

1 - 2 - 3 - 4 - 5 - 6 - 7 - 8 - 9 - 10 - 11 - 12
ducklings in the water.

Susie Mallard got all her ducklings out of the water and counted them once again.

1-2-3-4-5-6-7-8-9-10-11-12

ducklings on the bank.

She was not surprised when she realized that it was Jonah and Eve who were missing.

They were nowhere in sight!
Susie checked the water again hoping to find them there.

She searched through the tall grass
but did not find them there.

1 - 2 - 3 - 4 - 5 - 6 - 7 - 8 - 9 - 10 - 11 - 12

Susie stopped searching for her ducklings.
She needed God's help so she began to pray.
Susie knew that God could find them for her.

While Susie was still praying,
Jack asked Louise to help in the search for
Jonah and Eve.

Before long, God sent all her friends
to help Susie
find her lost ducklings.

They all began to
search..

Jonah! Eve! Where are you!?!

Drake joined the search too.

He was very angry that Jonah and Eve had disobeyed their mother.

Susie just wanted to find her ducklings safe. She knew she would forgive them, just as God always forgives her.

(Ref: Colossians 3:12-13)

Nothing good can come from disobedience!

Meanwhile, Jonah and Eve were having so much fun they did not hear their parents' calling their names.

First they found some rocks to play on.

Then they began to run through the soft green grass.

This was so much fun!
Much better than following their mother
around all day Jonah thought.

Eve was growing tired.
She laid down in the grass and began quacking,
"I am tired and I am hungry. I want my Mother!"

Ponder this:

A Susie's quack is much LOUDER than the soft quack of the Drake.

"You don't need her!" Jonah exclaimed.

"Drink some water. You will feel better. It is more fun for us to be on our own."

Eve followed Jonah into the water for a drink but she was beginning to wish she had never listened to him and disobeyed their mother.

Even though Jonah had fun for a while,
he secretly longed to see his mother too .

So Jonah and Eve began to search for their family.

They walked and
they searched
but they could not
find their mother
anywhere.

Jonah
and
Eve
had
lost
their
way.

They
both
began
to
wonder
why
they
chose
to
disobey
their
mother.

And then they heard something behind them.

"Oh please let that be our mother," they both prayed.

But THAT wasn't their mother!

Jonah and Eve
were so scared.
They hid behind the
closest tree but the goose
continued
to follow them.

Hank, the
honking goose,
was trying to help
them, not harm
them.

They didn't realize
he had been
helping with the search
for them all day and was
honking to tell the others
he had found
Jonah and Eve.

Ponder this:
Geese have approximately 10 different sounds to communicate depending on what they are trying to say.

Jack, Louise and Susie all heard Hank's honk.
They thanked God for answering their prayers and
began swimming gleefully toward the most
beautiful honking they had ever heard.

Drake heard Hank's honk from where he was searching and unfortunately for Jonah, got to him before his mother could arrive.

Jonah knew he was in trouble!
He had been scared when he was lost, but he was
even more scared of the punishment from
his father...

so he began to swim away from his father
as fast as he could.

Young man, do not resent it when God chastens
and corrects you, for His punishment is proof of His love.
Just as a father punishes a son he delights in to make him
better, so the LORD corrects you.
Proverbs 3:11-12 (TLB)

Jonah knew he could not avoid his father's punishment.

Eve had to be punished too.

As much as Jonah and Eve disliked punishment,
they both knew their father loved them enough
to try and teach them obedience
through his discipline.

Jonah and Eve were
sorry they had
disobeyed.

They were glad that their punishment from
their father was over and they swam quickly
back to the forgiveness of their mother.

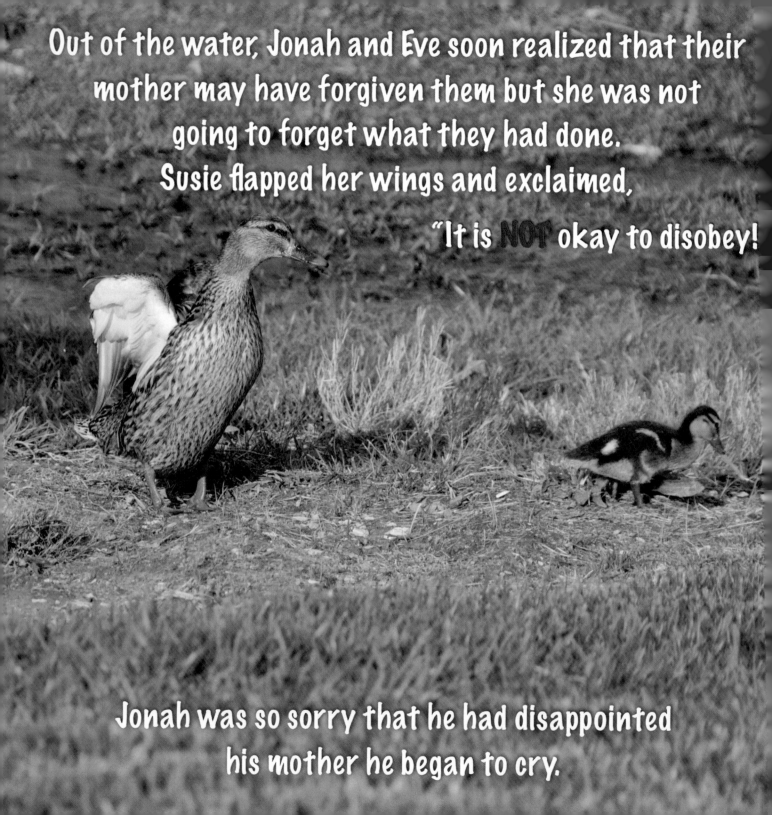

Out of the water, Jonah and Eve soon realized that their mother may have forgiven them but she was not going to forget what they had done.
Susie flapped her wings and exclaimed,

"It is NOT okay to disobey!

Jonah was so sorry that he had disappointed his mother he began to cry.

Forgiving her ducklings was easy for Susie. Especially when she saw how sorry they were for their disobedience.

Children must always obey their parents in order to please and obey God.

Obedience to God will protect you from making mistakes that you might regret later.

God loves you.
He will cover you with His feathers and shelter you with His wings. (Psalm 91:4)

Always Trust and Obey HIM.

Quack with JACK

1. Should you always obey your parents?

2. What are some consequences of disobedience?

3. Do you believe adults must obey God the way children obey their parents?

Be sure to read all the books in the Duck Ponder Series:

Book I

Will You be My Friend? (even IF I am different from you)

Book II

I Wish I was a Mallard...but God made me a Pekin instead

Book III

Hank the Honking Goose Learns to Listen

Book IV

Never FEAR! God is (always) near

Book V

Bully Be Gone!

Book VI

It is NOT Okay to Disobey

Coming soon:

Book VII — The Secret we are Dying to Know

CPSIA information can be obtained
at www.ICGtesting.com
Printed in the USA
398302LV00004B/9